Beale   JUN   9 '93

Exploring Science

The Exploring Science series is designed to familiarize young students with science topics taught in grades 4–9. The topics in each book are divided into knowledge and understanding sections, followed by exploration by means of simple projects or experiments. The topics are also sequenced from easiest to more complex, and should be worked through until the correct level of attainment for the age and ability of the student is reached. Carefully planned Test Yourself questions at the end of each topic allow the student to gain a sense of achievement on mastering the subject.

EXPLORING
PLANTS

Ed Catherall

RAINTREE
STECK-VAUGHN
L I B R A R Y
The Steck-Vaughn Company
Austin, Texas

Exploring Science

Library of Congress Cataloging-in-Publication Data

Catherall, Ed.
    Plants / written by Ed Catherall.
        p.   cm. — (Exploring science)
    Summary: Explores many aspects of the plant world, including the structure, functions, reproduction, and growth of plants. Includes projects and experiments.
    ISBN 0-8114-2601-7
    1. Plants—Juvenile literature.   2. Botany—Juvenile literature. [1. Plants.   2. Botany.   3. Plants—Experiments.   4. Botany—Experiments.   5. Experiments.]   I. Title   II. Series: Catherall, Ed. Exploring science.
QK49.C37   1992   91-40544
581—dc20   CIP
                                                               AC

Cover illustrations:
Left *Some seeds are dispersed by water. These coconuts, washed ashore, begin to germinate on the beach.*
Above right *A hummingbird seeks nectar. In doing so, it will accidentally collect some pollen from the flower. This pollen will be rubbed off when the hummingbird visits the next flower.*
Below right *A cross section to show the parts of a flower.*
Frontispiece *A spectacular display of zinnias in Beverly Hills, California.*

Editor: Elizabeth Spiers
Editor, American Edition: Susan Wilson
Series Designer: Ross George
Book Designer: Jenny Hughes

Typeset by Multifacit Graphics, Keyport, NJ
Printed in Italy by G. Canale & C.S.p.A.,Turin
Bound in the United States by Lake Book, Melrose Park, IL

1 2 3 4 5 6 7 8 9 0 Ca 96 95 94 93 92

Contents

PLANTS

There are more than one million different types of living things on earth. Most of the living things that you are familiar with belong to one of two large groups: the Animal Kingdom or the Plant Kingdom.

There is great variety in the Plant Kingdom. Some plants are almost too small to be seen without a magnifying glass. But some types of trees are the largest living things on earth. One such tree, the Australian gum tree, is shown below. Size is just one of the traits that make each plant well-suited for its own environment. Plants can live in places as hot as the Sahara desert or as cold as the Arctic.

Australian gum trees are among the largest members of the Plant Kingdom.

Plants differ from animals in many ways. Most animals move from place to place, and most plants do not. Plants usually continue to grow throughout their lives, and they are often green. But a more important difference is the way plants and animals get their food. Plants make their own food. Animals cannot make their own food—they must eat plants or other animals for food. Another important difference is the type of cells found in plants and animals.

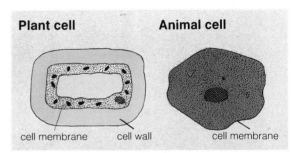

All plant cells are surrounded by a cell wall. Inside the cell is a chemical called chlorophyll, which absorbs energy from sunlight and makes it possible for plants to make food (see page 20). Animal cells do not have cell walls or chlorophyll.

Scientists divide plants into two main groups based on the way materials are carried through the plant. In complex plants, materials move through a system of tubes, like pipes in a plumbing system. Simple plants do not have these tubes.

Complex plants are divided into smaller groups based on the way the plant reproduces. The most complex plants are able to reproduce by forming seeds.

ACTIVITY
THE VARIETY OF LIFE

> YOU NEED
>
> - **a sheet of newspaper**
> - **a small trowel**
> - **a magnifying glass**

1 Go outside and find a suitable place to explore, such as the woods or a backyard.

2 Draw a simple map of the area and record the date.

3 Look carefully around you. List the different animals and plants that you see. If you do not know their names, give them descriptive names, such as "gray bird" or "tall tree."

4 Write down how many of each type of living thing you see.

Living thing		Number found
Animal	Plant	
grey bird		
	small bush with red flowers	
spider		

5 Look carefully at a small area of ground. List all the different plants and animals you find.

6 Spread out the newspaper. Using the trowel spread a little surface soil on the newspaper.

7 Look at the soil with a magnifying glass. Record any animals or plants that you see. Include any dead remains that you find.

8 Wild, natural places usually have more different kinds of plants than animals. Cultivated areas, such as gardens, usually have more animals than plants. Do your results agree with this?

> ## TEST YOURSELF
>
> **1.** Give two differences between animals and plants.
> **2.** What color are most plants?
> **3.** How do the most complex plants reproduce?

NONFLOWERING PLANTS

Billions of years ago, simple plantlike living things appeared in the ocean. They floated near the surface of the water where there was plenty of sunlight needed to make food. In time they formed huge colonies floating in the water. This same type of living thing exists today and is called algae. At one time algae were considered to be plants. But scientists classify simple algae as protists, not plants. Early forms of algal protists are the ancestors of plants. Some of these early plants colonized the land.

Like all simple nonflowering plants, these early land plants had no system of tubes to carry materials through the plant. As a result, they were small and

This fern fossil was found in Pennsylvania.

could only live in damp areas. Here water can move in and out of the individual cells of the plant. You may have seen mosses growing in damp and wooded areas. Mosses and liverworts are two of the few types of simple plants living today. Mosses grow in all parts of the world.

Eventually, more complex plants developed from early land plants. These plants had tubes that could carry materials to all parts of the plant. As a result, these more complex plants could live in drier areas and could grow to very large sizes. One type of early, yet complex nonflowering plant is the fern. Forests of huge fern trees were common during the age of the dinosaurs 200 million years ago.

The first seed plants arose hundreds of millions of years ago. During the age of dinosaurs, relatives of modern conifers, which bear seeds in cones, were abundant.

About 100 million years ago, the first flowering plants evolved. These plants had seeds that are inside fruits. From corn plants to maple trees, most of the plants that you see around you are flowering plants.

Liverworts are one type of simple plant. They grow in moist, shady areas, such as alongside brooks or on decaying trees.

ACTIVITY

LOOKING AT CONIFERS

> **YOU NEED**
> - a pine twig and pine cone
> - a leaf from a geranium or maple
> - a pine cone
> - a pair of scissors or a knife
> - a magnifying glass
> - paper and pencil

> WARNING: Be careful when using the knife.

Above *This Japanese larch is a conifer. This group appeared on Earth after the ferns.*

1 Look at the needles, or leaves, on the pine twig. How are these leaves different from the geranium leaf?
2 Cut a needle off the pine twig and examine it with a magnifying glass. Notice that, unlike a sewing needle, the pine needle is not round. Its flat sides hold moisture. How is this helpful for the pine tree?
3 Examine the pine cone. There are two types of cones. The male cone releases pollen; the female cone releases the seeds. Look at the scales. If they are spread apart, the pollen or seeds have already been released.
4 Break off a scale. Look at the scale through the magnifier. A small dark area at the base of the scale shows where the seed was attached.

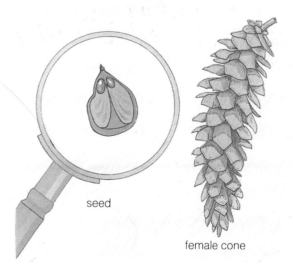

seed

female cone

5 Draw the pine needle, the pine cone, and a single scale. Label the area where a seed attaches to the scale.

TEST YOURSELF

1. What are algae and where do they usually live?
2. Why do simple plants live in damp areas?
3. What two types of large plants were growing during the age of dinosaurs?

SEED PLANTS

Until about 150 million years ago, the only plants on Earth were nonflowering. Then flowering plants started to appear, and today there are at least a quarter of a million different types in the world. They are found almost everywhere that life can exist, although most of them live in tropical regions, where it is very hot and moist all year round. All of them produce flowers. However, some flowers, such as those produced by grasses, do not look like flowers. Others have large colorful flowers. Some examples of flowering plants are grasses and most trees. Others are garden shrubs and flowers you have probably seen, such as roses, geraniums, and dandelions. All flowers produce seeds, which grow to make new plants.

There is a huge variety of flowering plants. The smallest flowering plant is the duckweed, which floats on the surface of ponds and lakes and can be about the size of this letter **O**. The largest is the Australian gum tree (see page 6).

The oldest living seed plants are the giant redwoods of California. They are at least 4,000 years old and can grow 350 feet tall. These giant trees are so large that, in Yosemite, California, holes were once cut through the bases of some trunks so that cars could drive through.

Flowering plants can be very useful to us. Most of the plants that we eat belong to this group, although we do eat some nonflowering plants. We do not usually eat a whole plant, but parts of it: seeds such as nuts, cereals, peas, and beans, or leaves such as cabbage or lettuce. We also eat some roots, such as carrots, parsnips, beets, and turnips. Whenever you eat bread or pasta, you are eating the ground-up seeds of a flowering plant.

This is a giant sequoia, also known as a grizzly giant or California redwood. These trees are able to live longer than any other member of the Plant Kingdom. This one is in Yosemite National Park, California.

This plant, called rafflesia, produces the largest flowers found in the world. They can be as much as 39 inches in diameter.

CAUTION: Find out what poison ivy, poison oak, and poison sumac look like and avoid these plants.

ACTIVITY

MAKING A PLANT RECORD BOOK

YOU NEED

- **a scrapbook**
- **a ruler**
- **reference books of flowering plants**
- **a magnifying glass**

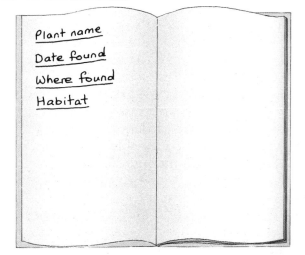

Plant name
Date found
Where found
Habitat

1 On each page of your scrapbook record information on a different type of flowering plant.
2 Use plant reference books to find out the name of each plant. Record the date and where you found each of the plants.
3 Write down their habitats: for example, meadow, forest, pond, or garden.
4 Draw and label each plant as accurately as you can. DO NOT DIG THEM UP.
5 With a magnifying glass, examine the flowers, leaves, stem, seeds, and any fruit.
6 Draw some parts of the plants in detail, such as one leaf or part of the stem.
7 Color all your drawings.

TEST YOURSELF

1. When did flowering plants first appear on Earth?
2. What is the function, or job, of flowers?
3. How can some flowering plants be useful to us? Give examples.

PLANT STRUCTURE

A single plant may be made up of millions of cells. There are many different types of cells. Each cell type has a particular task to perform. Plant cells of the same type work together and form layers called tissues. An example of a tissue is the tubes that carry water through the plant.

Several different types of tissues usually work together, and form an organ. In flowering plants, there are six different organs: roots, stems, leaves, flowers, fruits, and seeds. Each one has its own special task to perform for the plant. The roots hold the plant firmly in the ground, so that it is not blown away. Try pulling a weed out of the ground, and you will see how strong its roots are. Roots also take in water and minerals (chemicals found in the soil) for the whole plant to use.

A diagram showing plant structure. Insets show tissues and cells.

The stems of a plant can be compared to your skeleton. They help to support the parts of the plant that are aboveground and hold the leaves up to the light. They also contain the tubes that carry food and water through the plant.

Leaves have a very important task — they make the food for the whole plant. They have pores, or holes, in their surfaces, so that air that the plant needs can pass in and waste gases can pass out. These pores, called stomata, also give off water that the plant does not need as vapor.

Flowers play a special role in reproduction. When reproduction is successful, part of the flower becomes the fruit and seeds. The fruit provides protection for the seeds that will grow into new plants. A seed contains the embryo plant and its food store. This is used by the new plant to grow before it can start making its own food.

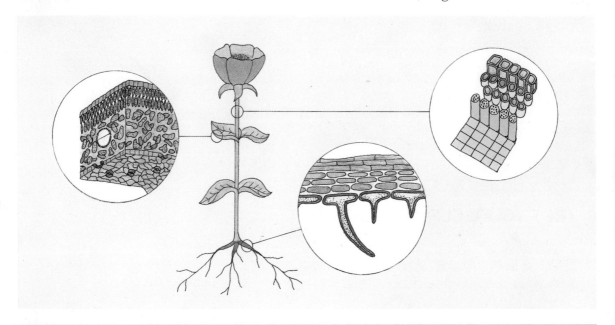

ACTIVITY

LOOKING AT PLANT TISSUE

> YOU NEED
>
> - **an onion**
> - **tweezers**
> - **a glass slide**
> - **a magnifying glass**
> - **a knife**
> - **a cutting board**
> - **a dropper (pipette)**

> WARNING: Be very careful when using the knife.

1 Cut the onion in half.
2. Remove one layer from the onion. This layer is covered by a thin tissue of cells forming a skin one cell thick.
3 Use tweezers to remove a piece of this tissue. It is usually easiest to remove a piece from the inner surface.

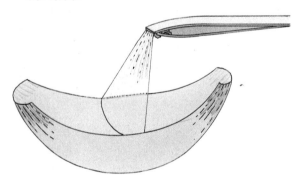

4 Put this tissue in a drop of water on a glass slide. Look at it through the magnifier. You should be able to see all the cells fitting together like tiles on a wall.

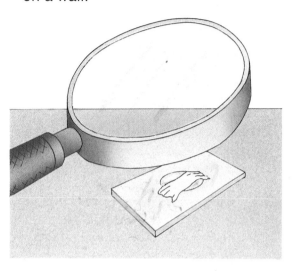

5 Draw what you see. Look at other pieces of tissue and compare them. If you have a microscope, you can see more detail.

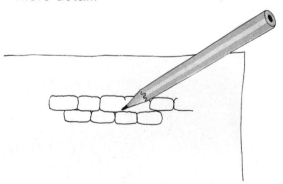

TEST YOURSELF

I. Give an example of a plant tissue. What is it made up of?
2. What is an organ? Name three plant organs.
3. No flowering plants consist of only one cell. Why do you think this is so?

ROOTS

Like animals, plants need water in order to live. Living plant cells contain water, in which is dissolved the food and mineral salts that the plant needs for growth, energy, and good health. Plants also need water to make food (see page 20) and as a transport system for carrying food, minerals, and gases through the plant.

Most plants get their water from rain that has soaked into the soil. The roots grow down into the soil, and tiny root hairs on their surfaces absorb the water and minerals that are found between the soil particles.

There are two main types of root. One type has a single, thick root called a tap root, with smaller roots growing out of it. These smaller roots help to anchor the plant firmly in the ground and are covered with root hairs. To carry the water away from, and food to, the roots, there are tubes that run down the center of the tap root and branch off into the side roots. You can see this clearly if you cut an old carrot lengthwise. Some tap roots, such as those found in the carrot, parsnip, and beet, are swollen with stored food. The stored food can then be used by the plant.

Above The orange-colored tap root of the carrot plant is a food store. Thin, pale side roots anchor the plant in the soil and absorb water and minerals from the soil.

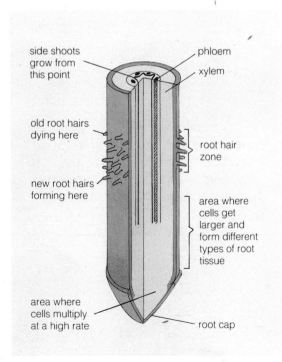

side shoots grow from this point

phloem

xylem

old root hairs dying here

root hair zone

new root hairs forming here

area where cells get larger and form different types of root tissue

area where cells multiply at a high rate

root cap

Left A diagram of a root.

Other plants, such as grasses and buttercups, have masses of thin, spreading roots called fibrous roots. Trees and other tall plants have huge fibrous root systems, reaching as deep as 50 feet underground. These roots anchor the plant and absorb the enormous quantities of water that the tree needs. This can be as much as 80 gallons every day.

Near the tip of each root is an area of growing cells. It is just below the area that produces root hairs. The growing region of the plant constantly divides into more cells, so that the root continues to grow down into the soil. As the root grows, it is protected by the root cap, which is a group of very tough cells covering the very tip of the root.

ACTIVITY

LOOKING AT PLANT ROOTS

YOU NEED

- **a trowel**
- **dandelions, grass, and a few weeds**
- **a bucket of water**
- **plastic sheeting**
- **a magnifying glass**

1 Use the trowel to dig up a dandelion. Carefully wash the soil off the dandelion root.

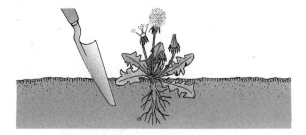

2 Place the washed dandelion on the plastic sheeting.
3 Dig up a tuft of grass. Wash its roots carefully and place it beside the dandelion.
4 Use the magnifier to look at both roots. List the visible differences. Draw both plants.

	DIFFERENCES		
	Type of root	Shape of root	
Grass			
Dandelion			

5 Dig up a few weeds and wash their roots. Examine the roots with the magnifier, then draw them.
6 Sort all your roots into two groups: those with tap roots and those with fibrous roots.

TEST YOURSELF

1. What are the two functions, or jobs, of roots?
2. What are the two main types of roots? Give examples of both.
3. Which part of a root absorbs water and minerals from the soil?

STEMS

The stem, or shoot, connects the rest of the plant to its roots. It usually grows aboveground and may have many branches, like those found in trees. The stem contains the main transport system of the plant. It contains two sets of tubes: the xylem and the phloem. The xylem transports water and minerals up the plant and the phloem transports dissolved food from the leaves to all parts.

Most plants have sturdy, upright stems that are strong enough to support the leaves and flowers, and flexible enough to bend in the wind without breaking. Some plants, such as trees and roses, form woody stems. The wood is made up of dead xylem tissue. Each season a new ring of xylem forms around the dead tissue.

Some flowering plants have stems that can support them. Bindweed gets its support by winding its stem around other plants, while strawberry stems grow along the ground. You may have seen ivy growing up the sides of houses and trees. This plant sends out special little roots that attach themselves to the wall or wood.

Stems come in many shapes and sizes: compare a tree trunk with the stem of a daisy. Stems may be rounded or ridged; smooth or rough; or covered with hairs or prickles, which help protect the plant from damage by insects and other animals.

If you cut open the stem of a dandelion, you will see the pith. This is spongy tissue in the center of the stem. It is surrounded by the tubes that carry food, water, and minerals. The pith often stores food that the plant has made. This food can be used when the plant cannot make its own food (see page 20), such as at night. Some flowering plants, such as the potato, have underground stems in which to store food.

Bindweed has a fragile stem, so the plant supports itself by twining around stronger plants.

ACTIVITY

YOU NEED

- **protective gloves**
- **a soft, green-stemmed plant**
- **a soft flower stem**
- **a rose stem**
- **pruning shears**
- **a magnifying glass**
- **poster paint**
- **a plastic cup**
- **white paper**
- **a soft pencil or crayon**
- **red food coloring and water**
- **a sharp knife**

WARNING: Wear protective gloves to investigate your plants. Also, be careful when using the knife.

1 Look at each stem with a magnifier. Draw what you see and describe it.

2 Use pruning shears to cut across the stem. Look at the cut end through a magnifier. Is there any water or sap oozing out? Can you see the tubes that carry food and water?

3 Put some thick poster paint into the plastic cup. Dip the cut ends of the stems into the paint, then make stem prints on the paper.

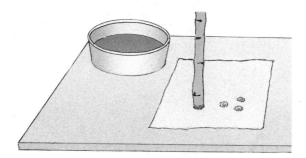

4 Investigate the bark on tree trunks. Place a sheet of paper against each trunk and rub over it with a soft pencil or crayon to make a bark print.

5 Stand the cut end of a flower stem in your plastic cup. Fill it with red food coloring and water to a depth of about 1 inch. Leave it for one day.

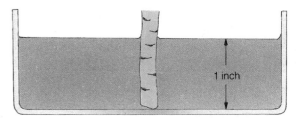

6 Take the stem out of the water and dry it. Cut through the stem at 1/4 inch intervals. You should see how the tubes have carried the water up the stem. How far has it traveled?

TEST YOURSELF

1. What tasks do stems perform?
2. What is
    the xylem?
    the phloem?
3. What is the pith? What does it do?

BUDS

A bud is one of the growth points of a plant, like that found near the tip of the root. In a bud, the cells are able to divide and grow larger; this adds extra parts to the plant.

There are two main types of buds: terminal and lateral buds. Terminal buds are found at the top of each plant stem, and allow it to grow taller. They may also form flowers when needed. Lateral buds are found in the angle between each leaf and its stem. They can grow into new branches or flowers. If the bud forms a flower, it is

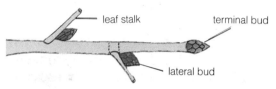

called a flower bud. Some lateral buds stay dormant (resting) and will grow only if the terminal bud is damaged: for example, if the tip of the plant is eaten by an animal. Gardeners often put this to good use. They will remove the terminal buds from plants to force the lateral buds to grow. In this way they can, for example, grow a bushy hedge.

Buds are not only a growing point, but are also a resting stage. They can stay dormant for a long time, until conditions are right for them to start growing. For example, the buds of deciduous trees, such as apple, maple, and sycamore, remain dormant in winter, when it is cold and icy. When spring comes, it is warm enough for growth to start again, and leaves, flowers, and new stems form.

Many plants live in areas with extremes of climate (very hot and dry or very cold), so their buds need protection. Buds also need to be protected from insect damage. This is why most buds are covered by a ring of leaflike structures called scale leaves. In a flower bud, the single ring of scale leaves, called sepals, forms the calyx. Protective scale leaves can be thick and waxy, covered in hairs (e.g., willow) or sticky like those of the horse chestnut. However, some buds are not protected, such as brussels sprouts.

A maple twig, showing leaf buds covered with protective scale leaves.

Horse chestnut leaf buds open. The scale leaves droop down and wither.

ACTIVITY

1 Cut a sprout in half lengthwise.
2 Cut another sprout in half crosswise.

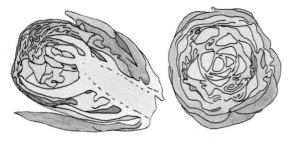

3 Examine each cut section of the sprouts with a magnifying glass and draw it.
4 Take another whole sprout. Use tweezers to remove the leaves carefully, one at a time. Work around the sprout. Record how many leaves you find. What happens to the size of the leaves as you work inward? What is left when all the leaves are gone?

5 Look at some winter twigs. Find and feel the buds. What are they like, and which trees are they from?

TEST YOURSELF

1. Where do terminal and lateral buds grow on a plant?
2. What happens to buds in winter?
3. Which kind of bud do sepals protect?
4. Why do most buds have protection?

MAKING FOOD

You have already learned that plants are able to make their own food. They need this food to give them energy and materials for growth. All plants contain a green chemical called chlorophyll ("chloro" = pale green and "phyll" = leaf), although not all plants are green. Copper beech, for example, has dark-red leaves, because the green of chlorophyll is masked by another colored substance.

Chlorophyll is able to absorb the energy from sunlight. This energy is used to turn simple chemicals (carbon dioxide gas from the air, and water from the soil) into chemicals called glucose, or sugar. Oxygen is given off as a waste product. We can show this in a simple equation:

$$\text{carbon dioxide} + \text{water} \xrightarrow{\text{energy}} \text{glucose} + \text{oxygen}$$

This process is called photosynthesis ("photo" = light and "synthesis" = joining together). Glucose dissolves easily in water, so it can be transported through the plant.

Most plants can join glucose molecules together to make starch. This does not dissolve in water, so it is often a good way of storing food for use when it cannot be made by photosynthesis. Biologists often test plants for starch, to see whether photosynthesis has taken place.

Most of a plant's chlorophyll is found in its leaves. The chlorophyll is collected in little disks called chloroplasts, found just inside the cell walls. These chloroplasts can move about the cell, depending on the position and strength of the sun.

bright sunlight

dim light

cell wall

chloroplasts end-on to the
light and evenly dispersed

chloroplasts broadside-on
to the light and collected
together towards brighter end

Above How chloroplasts move to catch the most sunlight.

Right Canadian pondweed cells under the microscope show the chloroplasts.

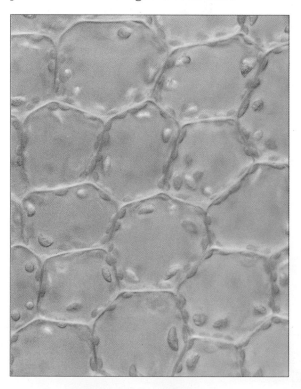

ACTIVITY

PHOTOSYNTHESIS

YOU NEED

- **living, clean pondweed (from a pet shop)**
- **a glass jar**
- **a glass funnel**
- **bottled water (carbonated is best)**
- **a small test tube**

1 Put the pondweed in the jar and place the funnel over it.

2 Pour in bottled water, so that it completely covers the funnel.

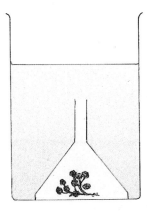

3 Fill the test tube to the brim with bottled water.

4 Cover the end of the test tube completely with your thumb. This will keep the water in the tube.

5 Turn the test tube upside down over the funnel, keeping your thumb over the end until the mouth of the test tube is under the water.

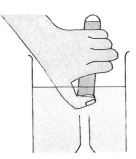

6 Leave the jar in direct sunlight for an hour, and watch what happens.

7 Look for bubbles forming on the leaves of the pondweed. Gradually, the bubbles should become larger until they float up into the test tube.

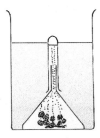

8 Put the pondweed in a dark place. What happens to the number of bubbles?

9 Now put the jar back in the light. What happens to the bubbles?

10 Use the information on page 20 to help explain what happened.

TEST YOURSELF

1. What gives green plants their color?
2. Describe the process of photosynthesis.
3. Where is most of a plant's chlorophyll found?

LEAF STRUCTURE AND FUNCTION

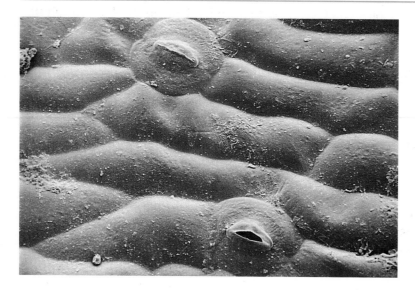

All true plants have leaves. They are very important to the plant because they are the main place in which photosynthesis occurs. Most leaves have a large surface area that turns toward the sun, absorbing as much light as possible.

Each leaf has three layers: the upper surface, the middle layer, and the lower surface. The upper surface is a single layer of cells that lets light through but protects the leaf from being damaged. It is covered by a waxy layer that stops water from being lost from inside the leaf. The middle of the leaf contains two types of cells. Just under the upper surface are the cells that contain most of the leaf's chlorophyll, so most of the food is made here. Below these cells is the spongy layer. There are large air spaces between the cells in this layer. The tubes (xylem and phloem) that carry water, minerals, and food are also found in this layer. In the lower surface, there are many holes, or

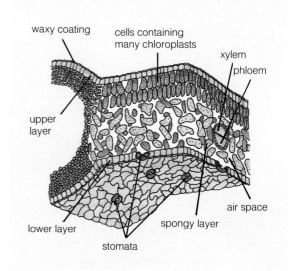

pores, called stomata. These allow gases to flow in and out. The plant takes in carbon dioxide from the air and gives out oxygen as the waste product of photosynthesis (see page 20). The stomata also allow water to evaporate. When it is very dry, the stomata can close and prevent moisture from being lost.

This water evaporation has a useful purpose. The plant needs water for photosynthesis, so water must get from the roots to the leaves. It must be "sucked" up the plant, often to a great height, such as in giant redwood trees. To create this suction pressure, water is evaporated from the leaves through the stomata, causing more water to be pulled up from the roots to replace the water that has been lost. This process is called transpiration.

Leaves can also store food, which can be used when the plant cannot make food. Examples of this are cabbage and lettuce leaves.

ACTIVITY

TRANSPIRATION

YOU NEED

- **a geranium or impatiens plant in a pot**
- **a plant saucer**
- **a large, see-through plastic bag (big enough to cover the whole plant)**
- **cellophane tape**

1 Water the plant thoroughly by pouring water into the saucer.

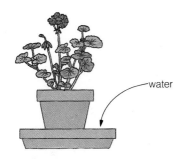
water

2 Put the plastic bag over the plant, and tape the open end of the bag to the pot. Also tape the bag around the bottom of the stems to keep water from evaporating into the air surrounding the leaves and stems.

3 Leave the plant in the light until the next day.
4 Look carefully at the inside of the top of the bag. Can you see any droplets of water on the bag?

TEST YOURSELF

1. What are the two main tasks that leaves perform?
2. What are stomata and what do they do?
3. What is the waste gas that is produced by photosynthesis?

MORE ABOUT LEAVES

There are two parts to a leaf: the leaf blade and the stalk. The leaf stalk contains the tubes that bring water and minerals to the leaf and food away from the leaf to the rest of the plant. The leaf blade contains smaller branches of these tubes, called veins, as well as the chlorophyll and other structures mentioned on page 22.

All leaves contain the same structures, but they have many different shapes and forms. Some plants have only one leaf on the end of each stalk, while others, such as mountain ash trees, have several small leaflets. In most leaves, there is a midrib, which runs down the middle of the leaf blade from the stalk and contains the main vein. Smaller veins branch off from the midrib: this type of leaf is called net-veined. Some leaves, such as grasses, have veins that run from bottom to top in parallel lines. Some leaves do not have a stalk.

The edges of many leaves are smooth, while others, such as oak leaves, have wavy edges. Roses and strawberries have jagged-edged leaves. Some plants have leaves covered with hairs or prickles that protect them from insects and animals. The cactus family is a good example.

Different shapes and forms of leaves found in South America.

Leaves can join the stem in different patterns. Some plants have leaves arranged in a rosette at the bottom of the stem, such as primrose. Beech trees have their leaves growing in a spiral up the stem, while privet has leaves on opposite sides of the stem. Still other plants have leaves that are arranged in whorls some distance up the stem (e.g., goose grass).

Leaves tend to be large and thin if the plant grows in a place where there is plenty of water. This allows a large surface area for transpiration (see page 23). Where water is scarce, leaves tend to be thick, so that they lose less water by transpiration.

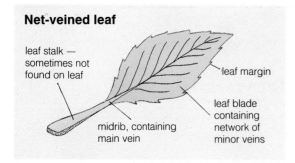

Net-veined leaf

leaf stalk — sometimes not found on leaf

leaf margin

midrib, containing main vein

leaf blade containing network of minor veins

rosette (leaves in a ring at ground level)

opposite

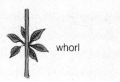

alternate (spiral)

whorl

ACTIVITY

LOOKING AT LEAVES

YOU NEED

- **a living plant with large leaves (or tree twigs)**
- **a magnifying glass**
- **a sharp knife**
- **a glass slide**
- **a dropper (pipette)**
- **a coverslip**
- **a microscope**

1 Look at the leaves on your plant or twig. Draw the leaf pattern and describe it.

2 Use the magnifier to look at the upper and lower surfaces of one leaf. List the differences.

3 Draw one leaf. Mark in the position of the midrib and the main veins.

4 Use the knife to peel off the lower skin of the leaf. Place a small piece on a glass slide. Add a drop of water and lower the coverslip on it.

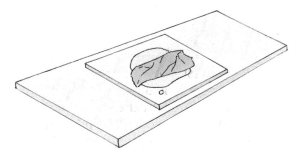

5 Look at your piece of leaf under the microscope. Can you see the stomata?

6 Repeat these steps with leaves from different plants.

WARNING: Be careful when using the knife, glass slide, and coverslip. Also, use care when touching hairy, prickly, or sharp leaves.

TEST YOURSELF

1. Describe and draw two leaf patterns.

2. Draw a parallel-veined leaf and a branching-veined leaf. Label the main parts.

3. Name two ways in which leaves are protected from insects and animals.

FOOD STORAGE

We use these parts of the plants shown above as food. This is because these parts contain the plants' stored food, so they are full of nourishment.

You know that plants make their food using sunlight, carbon dioxide, and water. Although carbon dioxide is always found in air, often water and sunlight are not available. During a drought, there may not be enough water to make food. Sunlight varies considerably: for example, photosynthesis cannot take place at night. In temperate climates (neither very hot nor very cold), winters have only a few hours of daylight, and this light may be very weak due to cloud cover. For these reasons, plants have to be able to store some of the food that they make when conditions are good for photosynthesis. This stored food can then be used when there is a lack of light or water. Young plants always need a food store that they can use before they are large enough to photosynthesize properly.

Food is usually concentrated before it is stored. For this reason, the storage space can be quite small. Plants turn simple sugars, such as glucose, into carbohydrates like starch. This is the main form of storing food and can be found in potatoes, cereals, and beans. Some plants concentrate their food into oils, as in peanuts and olives.

Food can be stored in the stems, leaves, or roots, depending on the type of plant. Celery and rhubarb have food stores in leaf stalks; cabbages and lettuce in their leaves. Onions store their food in bulbs at the bases of their leaves. Food is often stored underground: for example, radishes, carrots, parsnips, turnips, and beets store food in their roots. Swollen underground stems store food for potatoes and yams.

Seeds always contain food for young plants to use. The fruit that surrounds a seed is also full of stored food. (See page 36.) This often helps the seed to be carried away from its parent plant by animals and birds.

ACTIVITY

PLANT FOOD STORES

YOU NEED

- **a fresh old potato and old carrot**
- **two saucers**
- **water**

1 Wash the potato and the carrot very well to remove any chemicals applied to prevent growth.
2 Cut the top from the carrot, and cut the potato in half. Select the half that has more "eyes" (buds).
3 Put the carrot top in one saucer and the potato in the other. Fill both saucers with clean water.

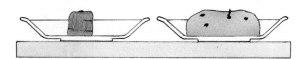

4 Put the saucers in a warm, dark place. This means that the carrot and potato will have to use their food stores to grow.

5 Look at your vegetables daily. Change the water often.
6 Draw and describe any growth that you see. In the dark, without light to help the plants make chlorophyll, any leaves that grow will be yellow.

	CHANGES			
	DATE	DATE	DATE	DATE
potato				
carrot				

7 Once the plants have grown a few leaves, put the saucers with the carrot and potato in the light. Record and try to explain the changes that you see.

TEST YOURSELF

1. Why do plants store food?
2. What is the main form of storage?
3. Why is food stored in seeds? Where else can plants store food?

RESPIRATION

This Australian mosquito fish takes in oxygen that is dissolved in the water. This oxygen has come from plants that also live in the water. Carbon dioxide is given out by the fish as waste and is used by the plants for photosynthesis.

You know that plants and animals get their energy from food. To do this, the energy in the food has to be released so that the living thing can use it. This process is called respiration and takes place in every living cell. When a piece of wood is burned, oxygen gas from the air is needed. It is the same with respiration: all living things have to take in oxygen to "burn" their food.

To show what happens inside each living cell, we can write a word equation:

carbohydrate ➡ carbon dioxide +
+ oxygen   water + ENERGY

This means that the living thing, whether it is a plant or an animal, uses oxygen to "burn" the carbohydrate in its food. Carbon dioxide is given out as waste, as is some water. It is easy to see this in animals, but more difficult in plants. This is because plants also take in their carbon dioxide for photosynthesis. It is easier to measure oxygen coming in and carbon dioxide coming out when the plant is in darkness. No carbon dioxide is taken in then for photosynthesis.

You know (see page 22) that carbon dioxide comes into the plant through the stomata in the leaves. Oxygen comes into the plant in the same way. It is dissolved in water and is then carried to every living cell in the plant. Roots get their oxygen from the air in soil. They also return their waste, carbon dioxide, to the soil.

Plants give out more oxygen than carbon dioxide, so this can be used by animals for respiration. In the same way, animals give out more carbon dioxide than oxygen, and this is used by plants for photosynthesis. This is part of what is called the "balance of nature." You can see this working in water: fish breathe in oxygen that comes mainly from water plants and return carbon dioxide, which is used by those plants for photosynthesis.

ACTIVITY
THE ENERGY IN PLANTS

YOU NEED

- **a small, shallow metal dish**
- **a large metal tray**
- **sand**
- **different vegetable oils**
- **scissors**
- **thin string**
- **matches**
- **a tin lid**
- **tongs**

WARNING: You must ask an adult to help you with this experiment.

1 Put the shallow metal dish in the middle of the large metal tray. Surround the dish with a layer of sand.

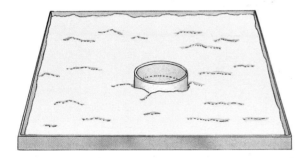

2 Pour one of the vegetable oils into the small dish.

3 Cut a short length of string and place it in the oil to act as a wick. Use a match to light the string.

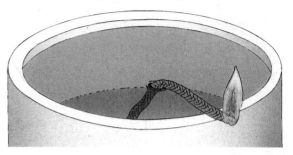

4 As the oil burns, you will notice that it gives out heat and light. These are types of energy and come from the energy in the oil.

5 Draw the flame. Look at the tip of the flame for signs of soot. This is unburned carbon from the oil. Using the tongs, hold the tin lid 2 inches above the flame. What appears on the surface of the lid?

6 Repeat your experiment using other oils.

TEST YOURSELF

1. Where does the energy in vegetable oil come from originally?
2. What is respiration?
3. How are respiration and photosynthesis linked?

VEGETATIVE REPRODUCTION

Although some plants, such as the giant redwood, can live for hundreds or thousands of years, no plant can live forever. They must be able to make new plants to replace the ones that die. Seed plants make new plants from seeds (see page 32), but many can also produce new plants in other ways.

Making new plants without seeds is called vegetative reproduction, or propagation. It is a good and quick method, because it means that the plant does not have to rely on insects, wind, or animals to help it make seeds. Also, the same type of plant may be grown from year to year, with exactly the same characteristics. This means that a particular kind can be maintained; gardeners use vegetative reproduction for good types of strawberry, apple, pear, potato, and many others. One drawback is that all the plants are subject to the same diseases as their parent. One of the most famous examples was a disease called blight that caused the Irish potato famine of 1845.

There are many types of vegetative reproduction. Some plants, such as daffodils, tulips, and onions, have an underground bulb that is full of stored food. Aboveground the leaves die off, and when conditions are right, new plants can grow from the bulb. Plants can also grow from a tuber (e.g., artichoke and potato). A tuber is an underground stem. When the plant dies aboveground, the tuber can grow into new plants. Other systems are shown in the chart below.

In some plants, sections of stem that are touching the ground form new roots. After a while the rooted stem can form a new plant. Plants such as ivy, periwinkle, and pachysandra produce many plants and cover large areas in this way.

Gardeners often take cuttings of plant stems and put them in new soil to grow copies of the parent plant. They can also put branch cuttings into slits in the stem of another plant of roughly the same type. This method is commonly used on fruit trees (such as apple, pear, and peach) and is called grafting.

Organ	Description	Examples
Rhizome	Underground, horizontal, branching stem, always swollen with stored food.	Iris, solomon's seal, couch-grass
Corn	Short, vertical, underground stem. Swollen with stored food.	Crocus, gladiolus
Suckers	Underground, lateral branches. Their ends turn up and produce buds.	Mint, pear
Runner	Lateral branches growing close to the ground. They grow rapidly along the ground, producing buds and roots at intervals. These become separate plants.	Strawberry, creeping buttercup
Stolon	When a weak stem falls over and touches the ground, its tip swells, it develops roots and further growth is continued by a lateral bud.	Blackberry
Root tubers	Swollen fibrous roots, each capable of developing a new plant.	Dahlia
Leaf buds	Bud detaches from leaf border and grows into new plant.	*Bryophyllum* (a leaf succulent. Buds grow around edges of leaves)

ACTIVITY

GROWING CUTTINGS

YOU NEED

- **empty yogurt cups**
- **a sharp knife**
- **plants such as impatiens, geranium, or ivy**
- **labels**
- **flower pots and saucers**
- **potting soil**

WARNING: Be very careful when using the knife.

1 Put a little water into each cup.
2 Use the knife to cut a small length of leafy stem from each plant. These cuttings should each be about 2 inches long.

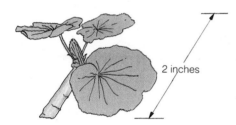

2 inches

3 Put each cutting into a different yogurt cup. Label each one with its name and the date.

4 Leave the cups in the light. Check the water level every day, and change the water every three days.

water

Name
Date

5 Watch the roots grow. When the roots are 3/4 inch long, plant the cutting in flower pots filled with potting soil. Label each flower pot.
6 Water your cuttings regularly by pouring water into the saucers under the flower pots. Do not overwater them.

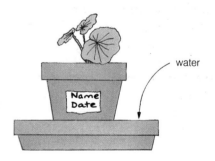

water

Name
Date

7 Make regular notes about each cutting's progress.

TEST YOURSELF

1. Name two ways in which plants make copies of themselves by vegetative reproduction.
2. What are the advantages of using vegetative reproduction? What are the disadvantages?
3. Describe how you would grow plants from cuttings.

FLOWERS

Apart from vegetative reproduction, flowering plants can make copies of themselves by sexual reproduction. Flowers are the organs that do this. They contain male and female cells that can join to make a new plant, which forms from a seed.

Each flower starts as a bud, which is protected by a ring of sepals called the calyx. When the flower grows, the sepals are forced apart, then wither and die. The petals inside are often colorful, although some flowers do not have petals. The ring of petals is called the corolla. In the center of the flower is the pistil. This contains the ovary, which is where the female cells are. These tiny eggs are called ovules. Out of each ovary comes a stalk called the style, which is usually sticky at the top to help it collect pollen. The top part is the stigma.

In most flowers, the male parts surround the pistil. They are called the stamens, and each one has a stalk called the filament. This holds up the anther, which is a pollen "bag" containing the male cells. When the pollen is ripe, the anther bursts and a pollen cloud is released into the air. There is usually more than one anther in each flower.

Flowers vary greatly in color, shape, and size. Flowers of grasses do not even look like flowers — they are tiny and have no petals. Most flowers are brightly colored, with a scent that attracts insects. Many have nectaries at the bottom of their petals. These produce a sugary liquid called nectar. Many petals have lines called bee guides to show insects where the

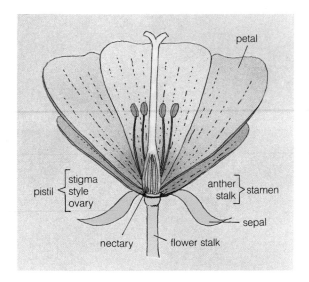

Above *Cross section of a flower.*
Below *Male catkins shedding pollen. These are found on alder trees.*

nectaries are. Some flowers have open, flat flowers, such as the daisy, while others, like the lily, have their petals joined to make a trumpet. Plants such as roses and tulips have only one flower on each stem. Others, like lupin, have a large cluster of flowers, called an inflorescence, on every stem.

ACTIVITY

Lupins have a large cluster of flowers, called an inflorescence, to attract insects.

WARNING: Be careful when using the sharp knife.

1 Draw one of your flowers: once from the side, then by looking down into it. Identify the parts and label your drawing.

2 Dissect (cut into parts) one flower, by first removing the sepals. Count the sepals and draw one.

3 Next remove the petals. Count them and draw one. Look for the bee guides and the nectary, using the magnifying glass.

4 Use tweezers to remove the stamens. Look at one with the magnifying glass. Draw it. Identify the filament and anther.

5 Use the pin to release the pollen from inside the anther. What does it look like?

6 Count the pistils in the flower. Draw and label the parts.

7 Use a knife to cut carefully across the ovary. Draw the section, showing how many segments there are. You will need a magnifying glass to see this. Draw the ovules inside. Notice how they are arranged.

8 Dissect other flowers and record your results. Compare flowers.

TEST YOURSELF

1. What is the corolla of a flower? Do all flowers have them?
2. Name the male and female organs of a flower.
3. Draw and label the parts of a flower.

POLLINATION

Sexual reproduction begins when the pollen from one flower lands on the stigma of another. This is called pollination. Sometimes, the pollen from one flower will land on the stigma of the same flower or of another flower on the same plant. This is called self-pollination, and is common in garden peas, for example. In most plants, the pollen is carried to flowers from different plants of the same type. This is cross-pollination and usually produces healthier plants than self-pollination. For this reason, most plants restrict self-pollination in several ways. They can have "male" and "female" plants, or separate male and female flowers on the same plant. Others have stamens that ripen before the stigmas, so that the stigmas are not ready to catch pollen.

There are two types of cross-pollination: by insects and other animals and by the wind. Insect-pollinated flowers are usually brightly colored, with nectar and scent that helps to attract insects, such as bees, flies, and beetles, as well as larger animals, like hummingbirds, mice, and rats. As these creatures move into the flowers, they brush against the ripe anthers, and the pollen sticks to their bodies. When the insect or animal visits the next flower of the same type, some of the pollen sticks to the stigma. The pollen of these flowers is usually rough and sticky to help this process. Wind-pollinated flowers are usually dull and small, and are often found in large inflorescences. They are carried on long stalks high above the leaves, and their stamens and stigmas protrude from the flowers, so that they can easily be shaken by the wind. There is less of a chance of the pollen reaching stigmas than by insect pollination, which is why this type of flower always produces much more pollen. It is usually the wind-pollinated plants that give people "hay fever."

This singing honey eater is feeding on the nectar of a eucalyptus flower. In the process, it will pick up some pollen from the flower and transfer it to another.

ACTIVITY

1 Approach your insect-pollinated flowers so that your shadow does not disturb the insects.
2 Record which insects are visiting the flowers. Watch what they are doing. Can you tell how the pollen rubs off on the insects?
3 Look carefully to see which color seems to attract the most insects; whether tall flowers attract more insects than shorter flowers; whether scented flowers attract more insects than those without a scent. Describe how you found out, and record your results.
4 Use the magnifier to look at a grass inflorescence. Notice how the flowers are arranged on the stalk. How do the flowers compare with those that were insect-pollinated?
5 Gently blow on a stamen that protrudes from the flower. Catch the pollen on black paper and look at it with the magnifying glass.

Ripe flowers on timothy grass. The stigmas and stamens protrude from the petalless flowers.

6 Draw a grass inflorescence, including a ripe flower. Label the parts that you can see.

TEST YOURSELF

1. What are the two main methods of pollination?
2. How do nectaries on petals help pollination?
3. Why do you think grass flowers do not have large, colored petals?

SEEDS AND FRUITS

When a pollen grain lands on the stigma of the same kind of flower, the grain begins to grow. A sugary substance that the stigma gives out causes the growth. The coat of the pollen grain has tiny holes called pores, and a pollen tube grows out through one of them. The pollen tube grows down the style, carrying the male cell. Eventually, this tube reaches the ovary and grows through its wall. Then it grows through a hole in the ovule, called the micropyle. The end of the pollen tube breaks and the male cell comes out to join with the female cell. This is called fertilization.

Once fertilization has taken place, most of the flower parts wither away. Sometimes you can see the remains of them: for example, withered petals and sepals can be seen on an apple at the end opposite the stalk. The fertilized egg cell grows into a seed, which has a protective coat surrounding the young plant (embryo). The ovary becomes the fruit, which helps scatter the seeds. There are many different types of fruit: some are juicy and sweet, such as apples and cherries. Others are leathery (buttercups), woody (oaks), or dry and brittle (broad beans). Some fruits have only one seed, as in plums and cherries, while others have many, such as oranges, peas, tomatoes, and blackberries. In some plants, it is not only the ovary that makes the fruit: other parts of the flower, such as the style, may stay alive. These extra parts always have some function, such as forming hooks that cling to animals' fur, so that the seeds can be carried away.

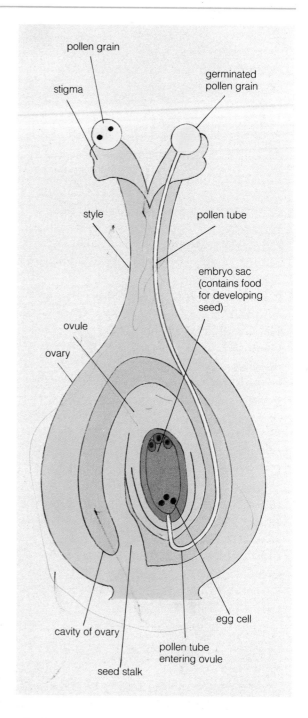

A diagram showing a growing pollen tube.

36

ACTIVITY

YOU NEED

- **a tomato**
- **an apple**
- **an orange**
- **a sharp knife**
- **a cutting board**
- **a magnifying glass**
- **fruits from wild plants**

WARNING: Be careful when using the sharp knife.

1 Examine all your fruits carefully. Now draw each one. The tomato and apple should still have the flower stalk and the remains of the sepals. Where are these parts?

2 Cut the apple in half along its length so that one half has the stalk at the bottom. Look at this half's cut surface. Draw it. Use the magnifier to see how the seeds are joined inside the ovary (fruit).

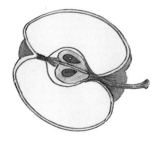

3 Examine your two other fruits in the same way. Draw the sections.

4 Look for fruits developing on wild flowering plants. Examine these fruits in the same way. Some of them will be very small, so you will need your magnifying glass to look inside the fruit for the seeds. Draw and record what you see.

blackberry

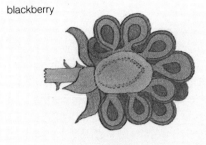

rosehip

poppy seed

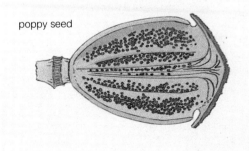

TEST YOURSELF

1. What happens during fertilization in flowers?
2. What happens to the ovary in a flower once fertilization has taken place?
3. Where is the plant embryo found?

SEED DISPERSAL

Seeds must be scattered (dispersed) as far away from their parent plant as possible. This is so that each seed will have enough space in which to grow without competing with other plants of the same type for water, minerals, and sunlight. There are several ways in which seeds can be dispersed.

Plants can spread their own seeds. Some have fruits that dry unevenly and spring open, catapulting out the seeds. Some examples of this type are pea, laburnum, and juniper. Others have fruits that open or develop holes, so that the seeds are shaken out when the wind blows, just as salt falls from a salt shaker. Poppy and grape hyacinth disperse their seeds in this way.

Many seeds have specially shaped fruits that can be carried away by the wind. Sycamore and ash trees have seeds with wings, while dandelion and thistle have "parachutes" attached to each seed. You may have blown the seeds from a dandelion flower.

Some seeds are carried far from the parent plant by animals that eat the fruits. Fruits are often sweet and juicy, such as cherries, apples, bananas, raspberries, and pears. The seeds inside these fruits cannot be broken down in the animal's gut, so they pass out in its droppings.

Some other seeds are dispersed by animals. Burdock and wood avens have burrs, fruits with little hooks, that catch in the fur of passing animals and rub off somewhere else.

Seeds can also be moved by animals in other ways. Seeds can be picked up in bits of mud that stick to the feet of birds and other animals. Other seeds, such as acorns, may be hoarded by squirrels and other small animals for a winter food store. The squirrels often forget where they have left their acorns, so some may start to grow the following spring.

A few seeds are dispersed by water. The fruit has a spongy layer that traps air, causing it to float. The best-known example of this is the coconut.

Burrs from burdock hook onto a dog's fur and are carried away from the parent plant.

ACTIVITY

YOU NEED

- **plastic bags**
- **a magnifying glass**
- **a yardstick**

1 Collect ripe fruits from outside. Take only one of each, to allow the others the chance to grow. Put the fruits into plastic bags.
2 Sort your fruits according to the way each disperses its seeds. Use the information you learned on page 38 to help you.
3 Draw and label each fruit.
4 If you have found any wind-dispersed fruits, test them. Mark a starting point, then use your yardstick to measure a 3-foot height. Drop your fruits one at a time from this height. It is best to do this experiment indoors so that there are no sudden gusts of wind to spoil your results. Be sure the fruits do not stain anything.

Thistle seeds are carried away from the parent plant by floating parachutes.

5 When the fruits reach the ground, measure how far each has "flown" from the starting point. Describe how each fruit flew. Which fruit was the best flier?

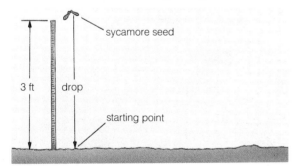

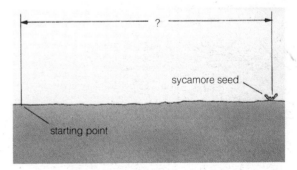

TEST YOURSELF

1. Why do seeds need to be dispersed?
2. Describe two ways in which seeds are specially suited to wind dispersal.
3. Describe two ways in which animals disperse seeds.

GERMINATION

Every seed contains an embryo (unborn) plant. This has a tiny shoot, a tiny root, and either one or two cotyledons, which are swollen seed-leaves. Seeds that have one cotyledon will grow into a plant such as corn, grass, or palm, while those that have two will grow into one of many types of trees and bushes or vegetable and bedding plants.

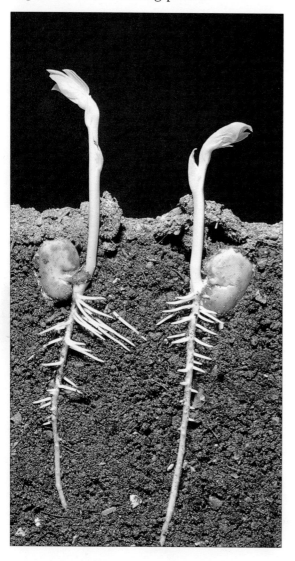

Seeds rest (stay dormant) until conditions are right. They may need to do this for many years, which is why they have protective coats. While they are dormant, seeds use very little energy, so they do not need much food.

Seeds need water, air, warmth, and the right kind of soil before they can grow into new plants. Warmth triggers many seeds to start growth. Seeds dispersed in autumn in temperate climates will stay dormant through the cold winter and will start to grow in spring. This start of growth from the seed is called germination.

When conditions are right for germination, the seed absorbs water through a tiny hole in its coat (the micropyle) and swells. It uses the food stored in its cotyledons to grow and eventually splits its coat. First, the tiny root grows down into the soil, allowing the young plant to take up more water. Then the tiny stem grows up through the soil toward the light. The cotyledons will either grow up with the shoot to become the first green leaves or stay underground. They shrivel and die once the food store has been used up. Once the shoot is aboveground, it turns green and produces its first true leaves. This means that the plant can now start photosynthesizing to produce food.

When conditions are right for germination, broad bean seeds put out tiny roots that grow down into the soil. A shoot pushes up through the soil. Aboveground, it grows leaves and will provide food for the growing plant.

ACTIVITY

YOU NEED

- **bean seeds**
- **a roll of paper towels**
- **a tall glass jar**
- **sifted soil**

Section through a corn seed

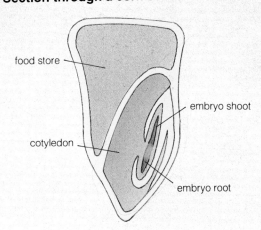

1 Soak the beans in warm water overnight.
2 Put a cylinder made from several paper towels inside the jar.

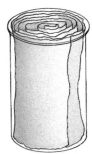

3 Put a small amount of sifted soil into the bottom of the jar.

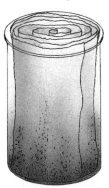

4 Slip the beans between the paper and the jar, pushing the beans down as far as they will go. Water the soil lightly.

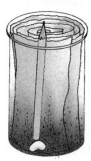

5 Put the jar in a warm, dark place. Look at the beans every day, water them, and record their growth. Look for the fuzz of root hairs. Once the beans have started to produce leaves, put the jar in a bright window. Measure their growth, and record any new parts that appear.

TEST YOURSELF

1. What is germination?
2. Draw and label a growing seed.
3. What are cotyledons, and what do they do?

PLANTS AND THE SEASONS

Because flowering plants need warmth and water for growth, the seasons have a great effect on them. Some parts of the world do not have seasons. In the tropics, for example, it is warm and moist all year round. This means that most of the flowering plants that live in those areas can grow and produce flowers and seeds at any time of year, and their seeds can germinate at any time.

Temperate climates (see page 44) have four seasons: spring, summer, autumn, and winter. Usually, their winters are cold, so plants that grow in these climates have a resting (dormant)

In winter, the leaves of deciduous trees have fallen. The trees stay alive by using the food stored mainly in their trunks.

stage that allows the plant species to survive the bad conditions. There are three ways in which the plant can do this; each way depends on how long the plant lives. Some plants, such as garden peas, live for only one year, so they are called annuals. The seeds germinate when conditions are good, and the plant dies shortly after the new crop of seeds is produced. These new seeds are the winter resting stage. They germinate the following spring.

Some plants are called biennials, which means that they live for two years. The seeds germinate in the first year, producing stems, roots, and leaves. In late autumn and winter the parts above the ground die, and the plant uses its underground food store to survive through the cold weather. The carrot is an example of this kind of plant. When spring arrives in the second year, the underground food store produces a new plant, which flowers. The plant dies after the seeds have been formed, and these are the resting stage for the second winter.

Many plants with woody stems (trees and shrubs) shed their leaves. These plants include the deciduous trees, such as the oak, ash, elm, and apple. In winter deciduous trees live on food stored mainly in their trunks. Some types of plants with soft stems also lose their leaves, as well as their stems, in winter; but they do not die. These plants are called perennials — they live for many years. Many perennials have underground bulbs, corms, tubers, or rhizomes (see page 30), which contain food stores that keep the plants alive in bad weather.

(see page 30)

TEST YOURSELF

1. How do annual plants cope with winter?
2. What is a biennial plant? Give an example.
3. What is a perennial plant? Give three examples.

These are the same trees shown opposite, but in summer. Now they can photosynthesize, grow, and store food to be used the following winter.

CLIMAX VEGETATION

The types of plants that live in a given area can change. When an area of land is first cleared, grasses will grow. Next, bushes may grow. These are often replaced by pine trees and later by such trees as oaks. The final type of plant growth is called the climax vegetation. It may take thousands of years for the climax vegetation to develop. The particular type of climax vegetation that develops depends on the kind of soil, the weather, and the amount of water available. For example, beech trees grow on chalky soil, while ash grows on limestone.

Forests do not grow everywhere, because trees need a great deal of water (see page 20). This means that the climax vegetation is different in deserts, such as the Sahara (a hot desert) and the Arctic (a cold desert).

There are also some "in-between" areas called grassland. There are two types: tropical and temperate grasslands. In tropical grassland, there is a short rainy season followed by a long drought. Temperate grasslands have cold winters with much ice and frost. Deserts and grasslands do not have many trees: their plants tend to be smaller, due to lack of water.

In many parts of the world, the climax vegetation has been destroyed by humans, to make space for farming, building, and mining. Once climax vegetation has been destroyed, there is a great deal of competition between any plants that grow there. Serious gardeners and farmers will tell you of the struggle they have to try to keep out "weeds," which can seriously damage or kill any cultivated plants.

Each year, vast areas of rain forest are destroyed for purposes such as building roads. This road is being constructed in Brazil.

The most serious damage done by humans to climax vegetation is the destruction of rain forests (called deforestation). Over the last 200 years, more than half the original area of rain forest has been converted into farmland and wasteland. Also, the timber can be sold for large amounts of money. Today, up to 50 acres are destroyed every minute.

This destruction has serious effects on the world and all living things. Local rainfall is controlled by rain forests; if they are removed, the area becomes dry and soil erodes until deserts form. They will never be replaced.

Floods, such as this one in Brazil, may become commonplace if the greenhouse effect is allowed to get worse.

Rain forests also control the world's weather patterns, particularly rainfall. They also use up a great deal of the carbon dioxide in the atmosphere (see page 20). If carbon dioxide builds up, and rainfall cycles are destroyed, the Earth's entire atmosphere will gradually warm up. This is called the greenhouse effect and could lead to the melting of the polar icecaps. This would cause sea levels to rise, flooding huge areas of land and killing many plants and animals.

TEST YOURSELF

1. Name four areas that have different climax vegetation.
2. On what does the type of climax vegetation depend?
3. Why, do you think, is it important to conserve (protect) rain forests?

Glossary

Atmosphere   The layer of gases that surrounds the Earth.

Bark   The covering of tree trunks.

Bulb   An underground bud. It is made from the bases of leaves, swollen with stored food.

Cactus   Fleshy desert plants whose stems can store great quantities of water. Stems also do the work of leaves.

Calyx   The group of leaflike structures that covers a flower bud.

Colonies   Large groups of animals or plants, often of one type, living together.

Conifers   Trees that do not shed their leaves in winter. They have small, needle-shaped leaves and cones. They are nonflowering plants.

Corm   A short, swollen underground stem.

Crops   Large quantities of cultivated plants growing in one place.

Cultivated   Plants that are grown and controlled specially, such as garden flowers and crops.

Deciduous   Plants (usually trees) that shed their leaves in winter.

Deforestation   The destruction of large areas of forest.

Desert   An area where very few plants grow, due to lack of available water. They can be hot, such as the Sahara, or cold, such as the Arctic.

Drought   A severe lack of rain or water.

Embryo   A young plant or animal before germination or growth.

Erosion   Eating away (of soil) by weather, water, wind, ice, etc.

Evaporation   When a liquid, such as water, is given off into the air as vapor (gas).

Famine   An extreme lack of food.

Greenhouse effect   The gradual warming up of the Earth's atmosphere, mainly due to large amounts of carbon dioxide in the air. This acts like the glass in a greenhouse, trapping the sun's rays inside the atmosphere.

Hay fever   An allergy to pollen. It causes sneezing, a runny nose, swollen eyes, and headache.

Legumes   Plants that have their fruits in pods.

Pasture   Land on which grass is grown so that animals can graze.

Rhizome   An underground stem that can produce roots and leafy shoots.

Sepal   One of the leaflike structures in a flower calyx.

Shrub   A low, woody plant, such as a bush. Shrubs usually have little or no trunk.

Temperate   A climate that is neither very hot nor very cold.

Tropical   Parts of the Earth between the Tropics of Cancer and Capricorn, which are imaginary lines on the Earth's surface. The tropics are always very hot.

Tuber   An underground swelling containing food stores. It can be in the form of a stem or a root.

Books to Read

Conserving Rain Forests, Martin Banks (Steck-Vaughn, 1990)

Discovering Flowering Plants, Jennifer Coldrey (Franklin Watts, 1987)

Flowering Plants, Alfred Leutscher (Franklin Watts, 1984)

From Flower to Flower: Animals and Pollination, Patricia Lauber (Crown, 1986)

How Seeds Travel, Cynthia Overbeck (Lerner, 1982)

Plant Life, Barbara Cork (EDC, 1984)

Plants, Lionel Bender (Franklin Watts, 1988)

Plants and Flowers, Brian Holley (Penworthy, 1985)

Plants, Seeds and Flowers, Louis Sabin (Troll, 1985)

The Tree Giants, Bill Schnieder (Falcon, 1988)

Picture Acknowledgments

The author and publishers would like to thank the following for allowing illustrations to be reproduced in this book: Eye Ubiquitous 26; Oxford Scientific Films *cover, frontispiece,* 6, 8, 9, 10, 11, 14, 16, 18, 19, 20, 22, 28, 32, 33, 34, 35, 36, 38, 39, 40, 42, 43; ZEFA 44, 45. All artwork is by Marilyn Clay. Cover artwork is by Jenny Hughes.

Index

First published in 1990 by
Wayland (Publishers) Ltd.
© Copyright 1990 Wayland
(Publishers) Ltd